Chinese Floral and Animal Charted Designs

Barbara Christopher

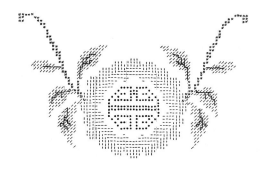

DOVER PUBLICATIONS, INC.
New York

Copyright © 1993 by Dover Publications, Inc.
All rights reserved under Pan American and International Copyright Conventions.

Published in Canada by General Publishing Company, Ltd., 30 Lesmill Road, Don Mills, Toronto, Ontario.
Published in the United Kingdom by Constable and Company, Ltd., 3 The Lanchesters, 162–164 Fulham Palace Road, London W6 9ER.

Chinese Floral and Animal Charted Designs is a new work, first published by Dover Publications, Inc., in 1993.

Manufactured in the United States of America
Dover Publications, Inc., 31 East 2nd Street, Mineola, N.Y. 11501

Library of Congress Cataloging-in-Publication Data

Christopher, Barbara.
    Chinese floral and animal charted designs / Barbara Christopher.
        p.   cm. — (Dover needlework series)
    ISBN 0-486-27537-X (pbk.)
    1. Embroidery—China—Patterns.   2. Decoration and ornament—Plant forms—China.   3. Decoration and ornament—Animal forms—China.   I. Title.   II. Series.
TT769.C6C47   1993
746.44′041—dc20   92-40611
                                                              CIP

Introduction

Chinese art and design have had a considerable influence on the decorative arts of the West, for the Far East has been a source of fascination for centuries. That fascination continues to the present day, fueled by the reopening of China to the West in recent years.

Here, Barbara Christopher presents a dazzling group of designs drawn from various Chinese sources. Dragons, lions, lotus blossoms, pandas, phoenixes and other motifs, both familiar and unfamiliar, make this a particularly versatile collection. Borders, corners and small spot motifs are offered, as well as large, full-page designs, so no matter what your project, you are sure to find a design to fit your purposes.

Most of these designs were originally created for counted cross-stitch, but they are easily translated into other needlework techniques. Keep in mind that the finished piece will not be the same size as the charted design unless you are working on fabric or canvas with the same number of threads per inch as the chart has squares per inch. With knitting and crocheting, the size will vary according to the number of stitches per inch.

COUNTED CROSS-STITCH

MATERIALS

1. **Needles.** A small blunt tapestry needle, No. 24 or No. 26.

2. **Fabric.** Evenweave linen, cotton, wool or synthetic fabrics all work well. The most popular fabrics are aida cloth, linen and hardanger cloth. Cotton aida is most commonly available in 18 threads-per-inch, 16 threads-per-inch, 14 threads-per-inch and 11 threads-per-inch (14-count is the most popular size). Evenweave linen comes in a variety of threads-per-inch. To work cross-stitch on linen involves a slightly different technique (see page 4). Thirty thread-per-inch linen will result in a stitch about the same size as 14-count aida. Hardanger cloth has 22 threads to the inch and is available in cotton or linen. The amount of fabric needed depends on the size of the cross-stitch design. To determine yardage, divide the number of stitches in the design by the thread-count of the fabric. For example: If a design 112 squares wide by 140 squares deep is worked on a 14-count fabric, divide 112 by 14 (= 8), and 140 by 14 (= 10). The design will measure 8″ × 10″. The same design worked on 22-count fabric measures about 5″ × 6½″. When cutting the fabric, be sure to allow at least 2″ of blank fabric all around the design for finishing.

3. **Threads and Yarns.** Six-strand embroidery floss, crewel wool, pearl cotton or metallic threads all work well for cross-stitch. DMC Embroidery Floss has been used to color-code the patterns in this volume. Several designs seem particularly suitable for the use of metallic threads; for these designs, appropriate colors of Balger★ #8 Metallic Braid have been suggested as a substitute for embroidery floss.

4. **Embroidery Hoop.** A wooden or plastic 4″, 5″ or 6″ round or oval hoop with a screw-type tension adjuster works best for cross-stitch.

5. **Scissors.** A pair of sharp embroidery scissors is essential to all embroidery.

PREPARING TO WORK

To prevent raveling, either whip stitch or machine-stitch the outer edges of the fabric.

Locate the exact center of the chart (many of the charts in this book have an arrow at the top or bottom and side; follow these arrows to their intersection to locate the chart center). Establish the center of the fabric by folding it in half first vertically, then horizontally. The center stitch of the chart falls where the creases of the fabric meet. Mark the fabric center with a basting thread.

It is best to begin cross-stitch at the top of the design. To establish the top, count the squares up from the center of the chart, and the corresponding number of holes up from the center of the fabric.

Place the fabric tautly in the embroidery hoop, for tension makes it easier to push the needle through the holes without piercing the fibers. While working continue to retighten the fabric as necessary.

When working with multiple strands (such as embroidery floss) always separate (strand) the thread before beginning to stitch. This one small step allows for better coverage of the fabric. When you need more than one thread in the needle, use separate strands and do not double the thread. (For example: If you need four strands, use four separated strands.) Thread has a nap (just as fabrics do) and can be felt to be smoother in one direction than the other. Always work with the nap (the smooth side) pointing down.

For 14-count aida and 30-count linen, work with two strands of six-strand floss. For more texture, use more thread; for a flatter look, use less thread.

★For information on where to obtain Balger threads, write to Kreinik Manufacturing Co., Inc., Dept. D2, P.O. Box 1966, Parkersburg, West Virginia 26102.

EMBROIDERY

To begin, fasten the thread with a waste knot and hold a short length of thread on the underside of the work, anchoring it with the first few stitches *(Diagram 1)*. When the thread end is securely in place, clip the knot.

DIAGRAM 1
Reverse side of work

To stitch, push the needle up through a hole in the fabric, cross the thread intersection (or square) on a left-to-right diagonal *(Diagram 2)*. Half the stitch is now completed.

DIAGRAM 2

Next, cross back, right to left, forming an X *(Diagram 3)*.

Work all the same color stitches on one row, then cross back, completing the X's *(Diagram 4)*.

DIAGRAM 3

DIAGRAM 4

Some needleworkers prefer to cross each stitch as they come to it. This method also works, but be sure all of the top stitches are slanted in the same direction. Isolated stitches must be crossed as they are worked. Vertical stitches are crossed as shown in *Diagram 5*.

DIAGRAM 5

At the top, work horizontal rows of a single color, left to right. This method allows you to go from an unoccupied space to an occupied space (working from an empty hole to a filled one), making ruffling of the floss less likely. Holes are used more than once, and all stitches "hold hands" unless a space is indicated on the chart. Hold the work upright throughout (do not turn as with many needlepoint stitches).

When carrying the thread from one area to another, run the needle under a few stitches on the wrong side. Do not carry thread across an open expanse of fabric as it will be visible from the front when the project is completed.

To end a color, weave in and out of the underside of the stitches, making a scallop stitch or two for extra security *(Diagram 6)*. When possible, end in the same direction in which you were working, jumping up a row if necessary *(Diagram 7)*. This prevents holes caused by stitches being pulled in two directions. Trim the thread ends closely and do not leave any tails or knots as they will show through the fabric when the work is completed.

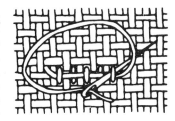

DIAGRAM 6
Reverse side of work

DIAGRAM 7
Reverse side of work

A number of other counted-thread stitches can be used in cross-stitch. Backstitch *(Diagram 8)* is used for outlines, face details and the like. It is worked from hole to hole, and may be stitched as a vertical, horizontal or diagonal line.

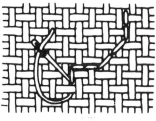

DIAGRAM 8

Straight stitch is worked from side to side over several threads *(Diagram 9)* and affords solid coverage.

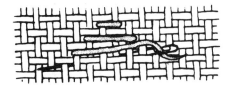

DIAGRAM 9

French knots *(Diagram 10)* are handy for special effects. They are worked in the same manner as on regular embroidery.

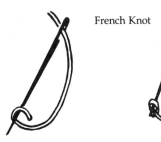

French Knot

DIAGRAM 10

Embroidery on Linen. Working on linen requires a slightly different technique. While evenweave linen is remarkably regular, there are always a few thick or thin threads. To keep the stitches even, cross-stitch is worked over two threads in each direction *(Diagram 11)*.

DIAGRAM 11

As you are working over more threads, linen affords a greater variation in stitches. A half-stitch can slant in either direction and is uncrossed. A three-quarters stitch is shown in *Diagram 12*.

DIAGRAM 12

Diagram 13 shows the backstitch worked on linen.

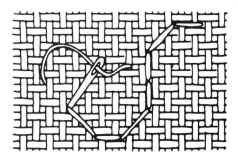

DIAGRAM 13

Embroidery on Gingham. Gingham and other checked fabrics can be used for cross-stitch. Using the fabric as a guide, work the stitches from corner to corner of each check.

Embroidery on Uneven-Weave Fabrics. If you wish to work cross-stitch on an uneven-weave fabric, baste a light-weight Penelope needlepoint canvas to the material. The design can then be stitched by working the cross-stitch over the double mesh of the canvas. When working in this manner, take care not to catch the threads of the canvas in the embroidery. After the cross-stitch is completed, remove the basting threads. With tweezers remove first the vertical threads, one strand at a time, of the needlepoint canvas, then the horizontal threads.

NEEDLEPOINT

One of the most common methods for working needlepoint is from a charted design. By simply viewing each square of a chart as a stitch on the canvas, the patterns quickly and easily translate from one technique to another.

MATERIALS

1. **Needles.** A blunt tapestry needle with a rounded tip and an elongated eye. The needle must clear the hole of the canvas without spreading the threads. For No. 10 canvas, a No. 18 needle works best.

2. **Canvas.** There are two distinct types of needlepoint canvas: single-mesh (mono canvas) and double-mesh (Penelope canvas). Single-mesh canvas, the more common of the two, is easier on the eyes as the spaces are slightly larger. Double-mesh canvas has two horizontal and two vertical threads forming each mesh. The latter is a very stable canvas on which the threads stay securely in place as the work progresses. Canvas is available in many sizes, from 5 mesh-per-inch to 18 mesh-per-inch, and even smaller. The number of mesh-per-inch will, of course, determine the dimensions of the finished needlepoint project. A 60 square × 120 square chart will measure 12″ × 24″ on 5 mesh-to-the-inch canvas, 5″ × 10″ on 12 mesh-to-the-inch canvas. The most common canvas size is 10 to the inch.

3. **Yarns.** Persian, crewel and tapestry yarns all work well on needlepoint canvas.

PREPARING TO WORK

Allow 1″ to 1½″ blank canvas all around. Bind the raw edges of the canvas with masking tape or machine-stitched double-fold bias tape.

There are few hard-and-fast rules on where to begin the design. It is best to complete the main motif, then fill in the background as the last step.

For any guidelines you wish to draw on the canvas, take care that your marking medium is waterproof. Nonsoluble inks, acrylic paints thinned with water so as not to clog the mesh, and waterproof felt-tip pens all work well. If unsure, experiment on a scrap of canvas.

When working with multiple strands (such as Persian yarn) always separate (strand) the yarn before beginning to stitch. This one small step allows for better coverage of the canvas. When you need more than one piece of yarn in the needle, use separate strands and do not double the yarn. For example: If you need two strands of 3-ply Persian yarn, use two separated strands. Yarn has a nap (just as fabrics do) and can be felt to be smoother in one direction than the other. Always work with the nap (the smooth side) pointing down.

For 5 mesh-to-the-canvas, use six strands of 3-ply yarn; for 10 mesh-to-the-inch canvas, use three strands of 3-ply yarn.

STITCHING

Cut yarn lengths 18″ long. Begin needlepoint by holding about 1″ of loose yarn on the wrong side of the work and working the first several stitches over the loose end to secure it. To end a piece of yarn, run it under several completed stitches on the wrong side of the work.

There are hundreds of needlepoint stitch variations, but tent stitch is universally considered to be *the* needlepoint stitch. The most familiar versions of tent stitch are half-cross stitch, continental stitch and basket-weave stitch.

Half-cross stitch *(Diagram 14)* is worked from left to right. The canvas is then turned around and the return row is again stitched from left to right. Holding the needle vertically, bring it to the front of the canvas

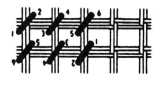

DIAGRAM 14

through the hole that will be the bottom of the first stitch. Keep the stitches loose for minimum distortion and good coverage. Half-cross stitch is best worked on a double-mesh canvas.

DIAGRAM 15

Continental stitch *(Diagram 15)* begins in the upper right-hand corner and is worked from right to left. The needle is slanted and always brought out a mesh ahead. The resulting stitch appears as a half-cross stitch on the front and as a slanting stitch on the back. When the row is complete, turn the canvas around to work the return row, continuing to stitch from right to left.

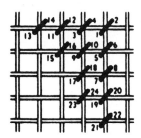

DIAGRAM 16

Basket-weave stitch *(Diagram 16)* begins in the upper right-hand corner with four continental stitches (two stitches worked horizontally across the top and two placed directly below the first stitch). Work diagonal rows, the first slanting up and across the canvas from right to left, and the next down and across the canvas from left to right. Moving down the canvas from left to right, the needle is in a vertical position; working in the opposite direction, the needle is horizontal. The rows interlock, creating a basket-weave pattern on the wrong side. If the stitch is not done properly, a faint ridge will show where the pattern was interrupted. On basket-weave stitch, always stop working in the middle of a row, rather than at the end, so that you will know in which direction you were working.

KNITTING

Charted designs can be worked into stockinette stitch as you are knitting, or they can be embroidered with duplicate stitch when the knitting is complete. For the former, wind the different colors of yarn on bobbins and work in the same manner as in Fair Isle knitting. A few quick Fair Isle tips: (1) Always bring up the new color yarn from under the dropped color to prevent holes. (2) Carry the color not in use loosely across the wrong side of the work, but not more than three or four stitches without twisting the yarns. If a color is not in use for more than seven or eight stitches, it is usually best to drop that color yarn and rejoin a new bobbin when the color is again needed.

CROCHET

There are a number of ways in which charts can be used for crochet. Among them are:

SINGLE CROCHET

Single crochet is often seen worked in multiple colors. When changing colors, always pick up the new color for the last yarn-over of the old color. The color not in use can be carried loosely across the back of the work for a few stitches, or you can work the single crochet over the unused color. The latter method makes for a neater appearance on the wrong side, but sometimes the old color peeks through the stitches. This method can also be applied to half-double crochet and double crochet, but keep in mind that the longer stitches will distort the design.

FILET CROCHET

This technique is nearly always worked from charts and uses only one color thread. The result is a solid-color piece with the design filled in and the background left as an open mesh. Care must be taken in selecting the design, as the longer stitch causes distortion.

AFGHAN CROCHET

The most common method here is cross-stitch worked over the afghan stitch. Complete the afghan crochet project. Then, following the chart for color placement, work cross-stitch over the squares of crochet.

OTHER CHARTED METHODS

Latch hook, Assisi embroidery, beading, cross-stitch on needlepoint canvas (a European favorite) and lace net embroidery are among the other needlework methods worked from charts.

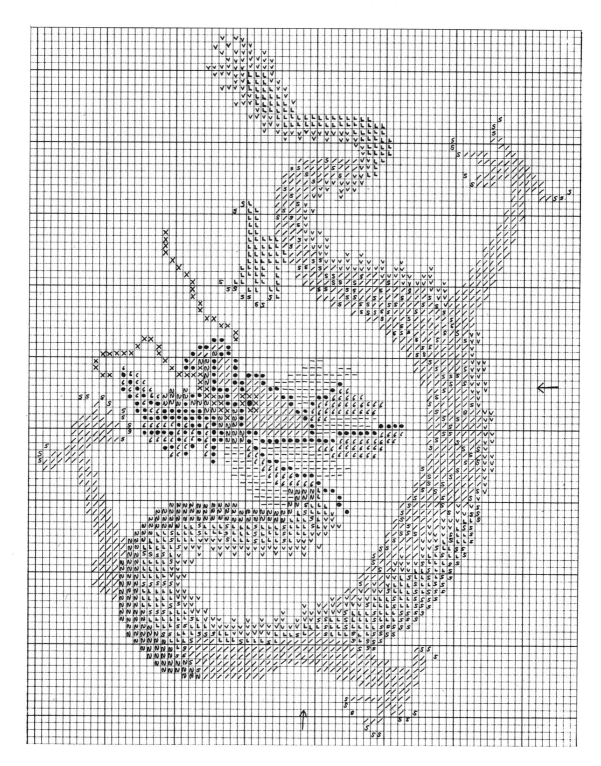

GOLDEN DRAGON

77 stitches by 98 stitches

18ct
4¼ × 5½

14ct
5½ × 7

	DMC #		BALGER or #8 BRAID	
S	300	very dark mahogany	2122	curry
X	666	bright Christmas red	003	red
⁄	725	topaz	002	gold
6	740	tangerine	027	orange
L	783	Christmas gold	021	copper
N	806	dark peacock blue	006	blue
●	816	garnet red	021HL	fuchsia
V	958	dark aqua	2829	sea foam
−	3766	light peacock blue	014HL	sky blue

Use either embroidery floss or metallic braid

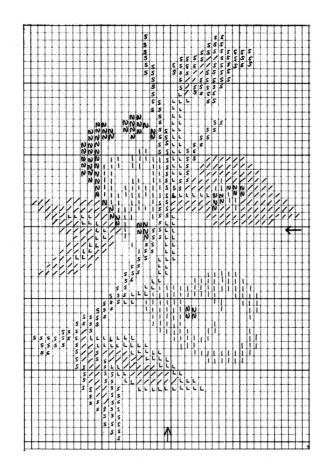

CITRON AND WEALTH ◀

39 stitches by 57 stitches

	DMC #	
L	518	light Wedgwood blue
6	580	dark moss green
I	604	light cranberry
N	666	bright Christmas red
/	704	bright chartreuse

18 — 2¼ × 3¼
14 — 2¾ × 4

18 — 2 × 2¼
14 — 2½ × 3

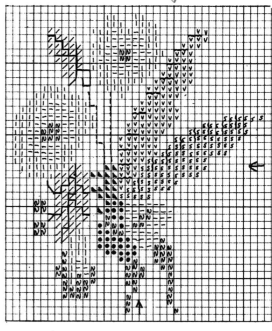

BUTTERFLY AND FLOWERS ▶

36 stitches by 42 stitches

BACK-STITCH	CROSS-STITCH	DMC #	
——		580	dark moss green
	−	604	light cranberry
	N	606	bright orange red
	/	704	bright chartreuse
	V	725	topaz
	6	783	Christmas gold
~~	●	801	dark coffee brown
– – – –	◣	3685	dark mauve
	I	3761	light sky blue

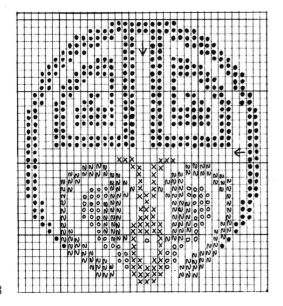

18 — 2 × 2¼
14 — 2½ × 3¾

BUTTERFLY AND JOY ◀

34 stitches by 37 stitches

	DMC #		BALGER or #8 BRAID	
●	310	black		
N	606	bright orange red		
□	729	medium old gold	002	gold
✕	995	dark electric blue		

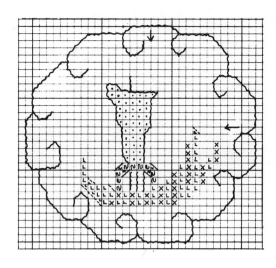

33 stitches by 30 stitches

18    $1\frac{3}{4} \times 2\frac{1}{4}$

14    $2\frac{1}{2} \times 2\frac{3}{4}$

BACK-STITCH	CROSS-STITCH	DMC #	
	⊡		white
∿∿		310	black
	☒	518	light Wedgwood blue
─────	Ν	606	bright orange red
‒ ‒ ‒ ‒	L	783	Christmas gold

GOLD DIAMOND ►

33 stitches by 33 stitches

	DMC #		BALGER or #8 BRAID	
Ν	321	Christmas red		
I	606	bright orange red		
⟋	725	topaz	002	gold
⊙	995	dark electric blue		

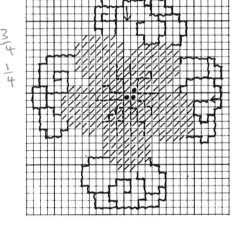

$1\frac{1}{2} \times 1\frac{3}{4}$

$2 \times 2\frac{1}{4}$

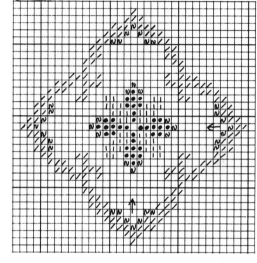

18 – 2×2

14   $2\frac{1}{2} \times 2\frac{1}{2}$

◄ RED FLOWER

27 stitches by 30 stitches

BACK-STITCH	CROSS-STITCH	DMC #	
	⟋	666	bright Christmas red
─────	⊙	816	garnet red
∿∿		820	very dark royal blue

CHRYSANTHEMUM BUDS ►

30 stitches by 39 stitches

BACK-STITCH	CROSS-STITCH	DMC #	
	Ν	352	light coral
	⟋	554	light violet
	◩	725	topaz

18    $1\frac{3}{4} \times 2\frac{1}{4}$

14    $2\frac{1}{4} \times 2\frac{3}{4}$

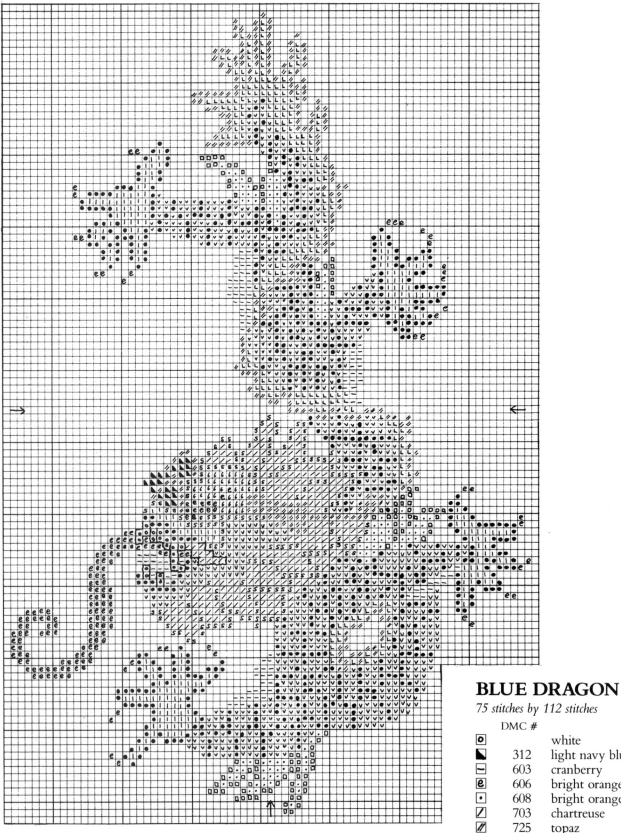

BLUE DRAGON
75 stitches by 112 stitches

	DMC #	
o		white
◼	312	light navy blue
⊟	603	cranberry
e	606	bright orange red
•	608	bright orange
/	703	chartreuse
⫽	725	topaz
●	939	very dark navy blue
▫	943	medium aquamarine
s	991	dark aquamarine
v	995	dark electric blue
L	996	medium electric blue
I	3761	light sky blue
⬗	3765	very dark peacock blue

18   4 $\frac{1}{4}$ x 6 $\frac{1}{4}$

14   5 $\frac{1}{2}$ x 8

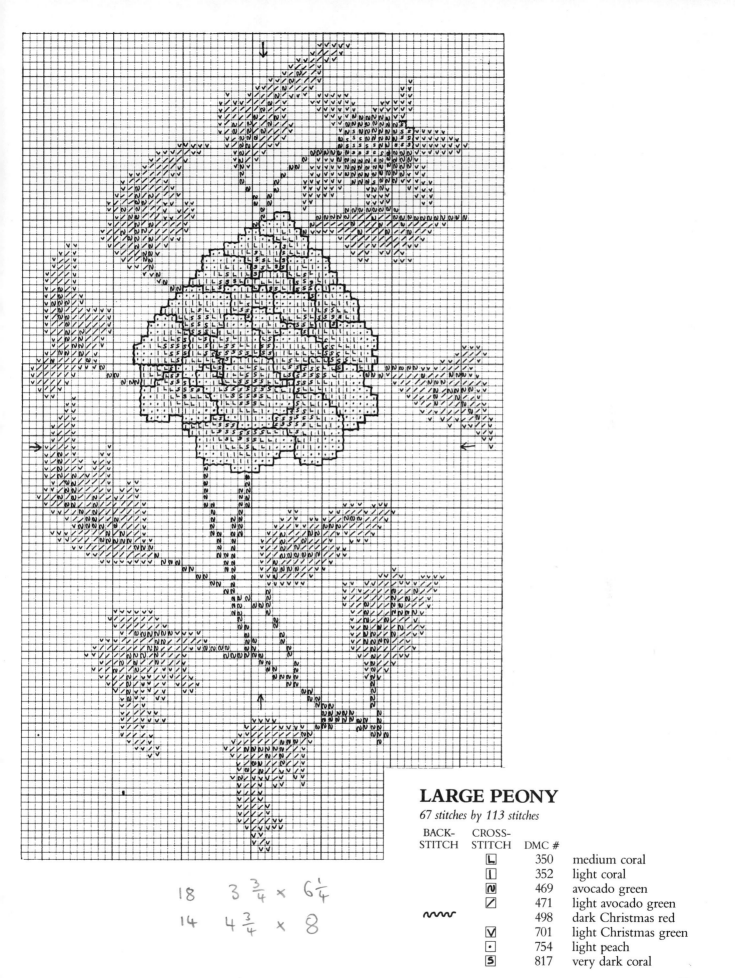

LARGE PEONY

67 stitches by 113 stitches

BACK-STITCH	CROSS-STITCH	DMC #	
	L	350	medium coral
	I	352	light coral
	N	469	avocado green
	/	471	light avocado green
∿		498	dark Christmas red
	V	701	light Christmas green
	·	754	light peach
	S	817	very dark coral

18   3 ¾ × 6 ¼

14   4 ¾ × 8

▲ LION

92 stitches by 86 stitches

BACK-STITCH	CROSS-STITCH	DMC #		or	BALGER #8 BRAID
══	●	310	black		
	―	604	light cranberry		
	L	666	bright Christmas red		
	•	725	topaz	002	gold
	▯	995	dark electric blue		
	⁄	996	medium electric blue		
	V	3761	light sky blue		

18    $5\frac{1}{4} \times 4\frac{3}{4}$

14    $6\frac{1}{2} \times 6$

FISH ▶

68 stitches by 81 stitches

	DMC #	
V	471	light avocado green
S	580	dark moss green
P	666	bright Christmas red
◣	699	Christmas green
‖	740	tangerine
―	741	medium tangerine
I	743	dark yellow
●	797	royal blue
L	806	dark peacock blue
X	807	medium peacock blue
N	815	medium garnet red
6	947	burnt orange
⁄	3766	light peacock blue

BUTTERFLY IN A FRAME ▶

37 stitches by 33 stitches

BACK-STITCH	CROSS-STITCH	DMC #	
∼∼∼	●	311	medium navy blue
	✗	333	dark lilac
	𝖨	351	coral
	╱	666	bright Christmas red
	L	725	topaz
	S	782	medium topaz
	ⁿ	806	dark peacock blue
	◣	816	garnet red
	·	3761	light sky blue

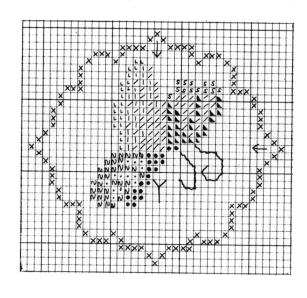

18 2 × 1¾

14 2¾ × 2¼

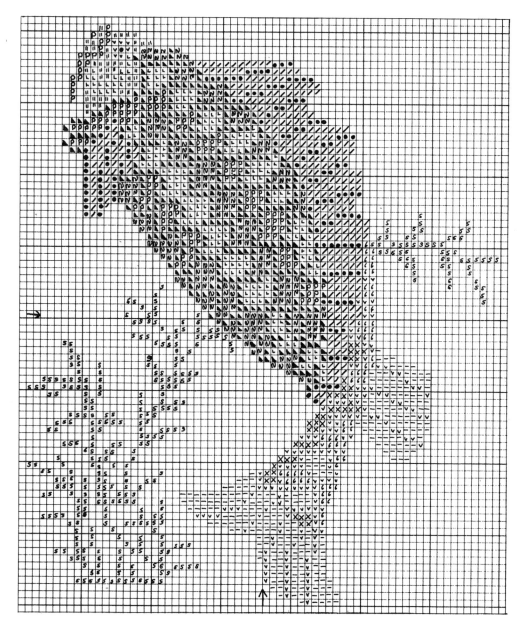

18 3¾ × 4½

14 4¾ × 3¾

13

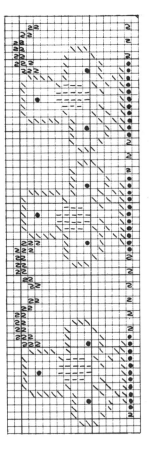

▲ RED AND BLUE BORDER

38 stitch repeat by 17 stitches

	DMC #	
◢	666	bright Christmas red
●	815	medium garnet red
I	996	medium electric blue
2	3765	very dark peacock blue

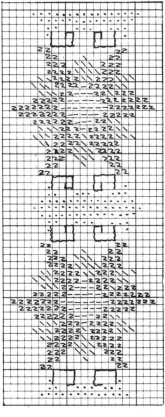

▲ BLUE AND GOLD BORDER

27 stitch repeat by 21 stitches

BACK-STITCH	CROSS-STITCH	DMC #	
	I	666	bright Christmas red
	◢	699	Christmas green
	•	913	medium Nile green
~~	2	972	yellow orange
		995	dark electric blue

▼ SERPENT

74 stitches by 41 stitches

	DMC #	
2	319	very dark pistachio green
II	608	bright orange
V	666	bright Christmas red
◹	704	bright chartreuse
S	782	medium topaz

18   4 × 2¼

14   5¼ × 3

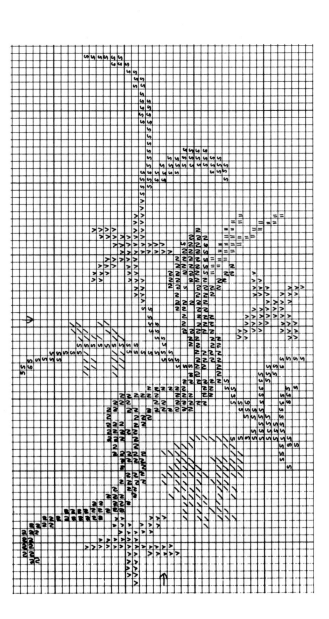

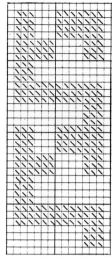

▲ GEOMETRIC BORDER

17 stitch repeat by 13 stitches

DMC #
◪	995	dark electric blue

▼ BRANCH OF FLOWERS

73 stitches by 30 stitches

DMC #
⊡	400	dark mahogany
L	703	chartreuse
⊿	729	medium old gold
❘	740	tangerine
V	807	medium peacock blue
N	3765	very dark peacock blue
❙	3766	light peacock blue

▲ FLOWER SPRAY

78 stitches by 52 stitches

DMC #
N	580	dark moss green
V	603	cranberry
❘	608	bright orange
❙	666	bright Christmas red
L	702	kelly green
⊿	704	bright chartreuse
X	815	medium garnet red
S	943	medium aquamarine

$18 \quad 4\frac{1}{4} \times 2\frac{3}{4}$

$14 \quad 5\frac{1}{2} \times 3\frac{3}{4}$

▼ MANDARIN DUCK

81 stitches by 81 stitches

BACK-STITCH	CROSS-STITCH	DMC #	
	◣	469	avocado green
	℮	666	bright Christmas red
	⁄	704	bright chartreuse
	V	725	topaz
	•	726	light topaz
	6	783	Christmas gold
∿∿∿	●	823	dark navy blue
– – –	S	910	dark emerald green
	P	943	medium aquamarine
	I	958	dark aqua
	＋	961	dark dusty pink
	N	995	dark electric blue
	–	3761	light sky blue
	L	3765	very dark peacock blue

18 4½ x 4½
14 5¾ x 5¾

PEACOCK ►

89 stitches by 61 stitches

BACK-STITCH	CROSS-STITCH	DMC #		or BALGER #8 BRAID	
——	●	310	black	005	black
	✕	420	dark hazelnut brown	034	confetti
∘∘∘∘∘	⊟	725	topaz	013	beige
– – – –	I	782	medium topaz	021	copper
∿∿∿	N	820	very dark royal blue	018	navy
═══	6	911	medium emerald green	008	green
	S	943	medium aquamarine	029	turquoise
⋯⋯⋯	⁄	955	light Nile green	044	confetti
	$	995	dark electric blue	006	blue
	V	996	medium electric blue	014	sky blue

Use either embroidery floss or metallic braid

18 5 x 3½

14 6½ x 4½

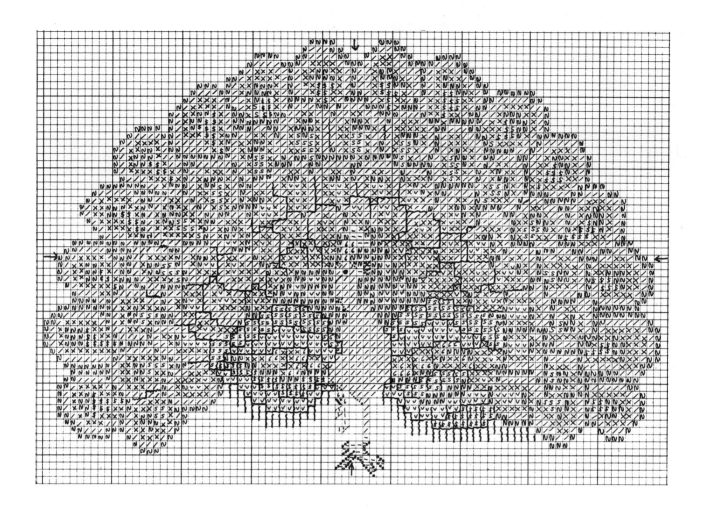

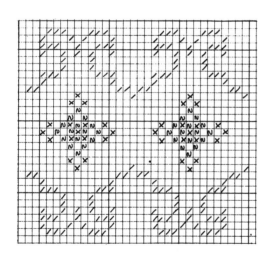

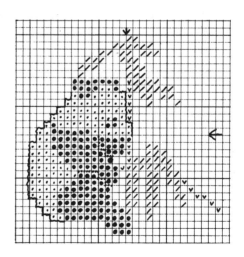

▲ FLOWER BORDER

16 stitch repeat by 29 stitches

	DMC #	
☒	666	bright Christmas red
⧄	725	topaz
N	995	dark electric blue

▲ PANDA

28 stitches by 28 stitches

BACK-STITCH	CROSS-STITCH	DMC #	
·······	⊡		white
∿∿∿	⊙	310	black
	V	700	bright Christmas green
	⧄	704	bright chartreuse

18   1½ × 1½

14   2 × 2

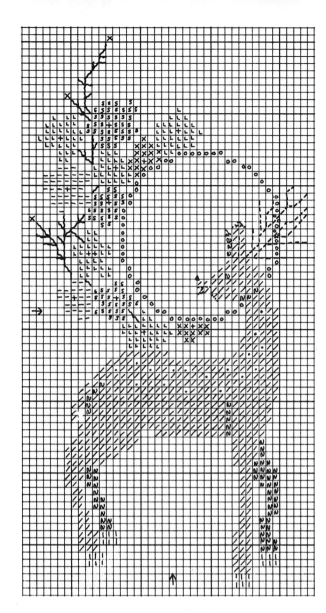

◄ DEER
40 stitches by 77 stitches

FRENCH KNOT	BACK-STITCH	CROSS-STITCH	DMC #	
△	– – –	Ν	434	light brown
	••••••	∕	437	light tan
		⊟	601	dark cranberry
		Χ	602	medium cranberry
		S	666	bright Christmas red
	∿∿∿		700	bright Christmas green
		⊞	704	bright chartreuse
		·	712	cream
		▯	739	fawn beige
		o	743	dark yellow
		L	3716	light dusty pink

18 $2\frac{1}{4} \times 4\frac{1}{4}$

14 $2\frac{3}{4} \times 5\frac{1}{2}$

▼ TINY BIRD
69 stitches by 46 stitches

BACK-STITCH	CROSS-STITCH	DMC #	
	∕	603	cranberry
	S	666	bright Christmas red
———	▯	742	light tangerine
	V	807	medium peacock blue
∿∿∿	·	938	ultra dark coffee brown
	Ν	3345	dark hunter green

18 $3\frac{3}{4} \times 2\frac{1}{2}$

14 $5 \times 3\frac{1}{4}$

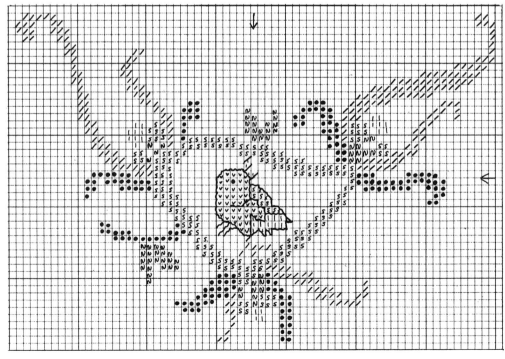

18 3½ × 2½

14 4½ × 3¼

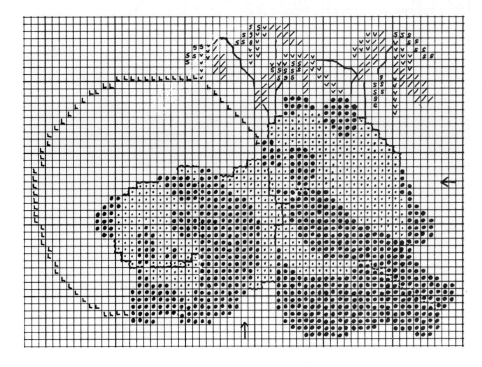

▲ TWO PANDAS

61 stitches by 44 stitches

BACK-STITCH	CROSS-STITCH	DMC #	
– – – –	⊡		white
∿∿∿	⬤	310	black
	S	469	avocado green
	∕	471	light avocado green
	Ⓝ	701	light Christmas green
	V	704	bright chartreuse
	L	740	tangerine

▼ BIRD AND PAGODA

72 stitches by 46 stitches

BACK-STITCH	CROSS-STITCH	DMC #	
∿∿∿	⬤	310	black
	⊟	606	bright orange red
	∕	704	bright chartreuse
	V	783	Christmas gold
	⊟	995	dark electric blue
	⊡	996	medium electric blue

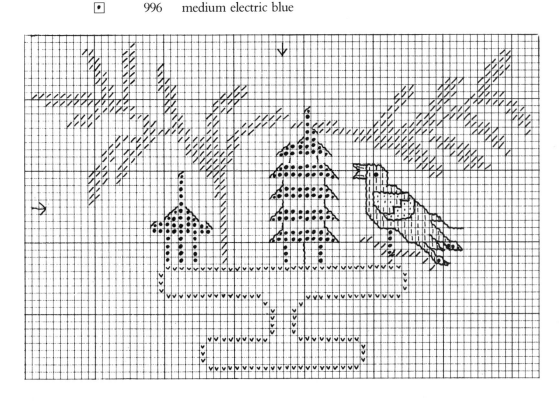

18 4 × 2½

14 5¼ × 3¼

BLACK DRAGON

93 stitches by 111 stitches

BACK-STITCH	CROSS-STITCH	DMC #		or	BALGER #8 BRAID	
	●	310	black			
	S	725	topaz		002	gold
	╱	995	dark electric blue			
	I	996	medium electric blue			

18 $5\frac{1}{4} \times 6\frac{1}{4}$

14 $6\frac{3}{4} \times 8$

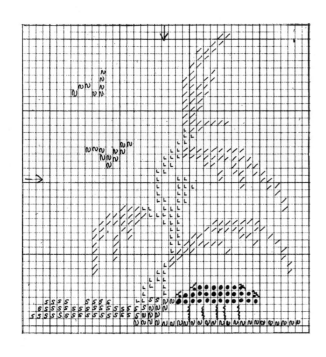

◄ LANDSCAPE

39 stitches by 41 stitches

BACK-STITCH	CROSS-STITCH	DMC #	
	●	310	black
	╱	704	bright chartreuse
	S	912	light emerald green
	∾	975	dark golden brown
	L	976	medium golden brown

PERSIMMON ►

42 stitches by 47 stitches

18 $2\frac{1}{4} \times 2\frac{3}{4}$

14 $3 \times 3\frac{1}{4}$

	DMC #	
I	608	bright orange
─	666	bright Christmas red
∾	699	Christmas green
╱	702	kelly green
·	742	light tangerine

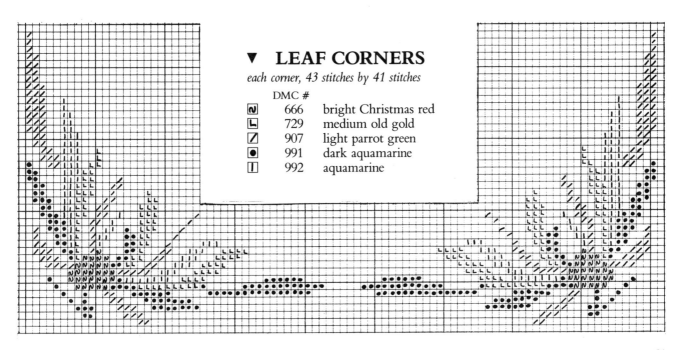

▼ LEAF CORNERS

each corner, 43 stitches by 41 stitches

	DMC #	
∾	666	bright Christmas red
L	729	medium old gold
╱	907	light parrot green
●	991	dark aquamarine
I	992	aquamarine

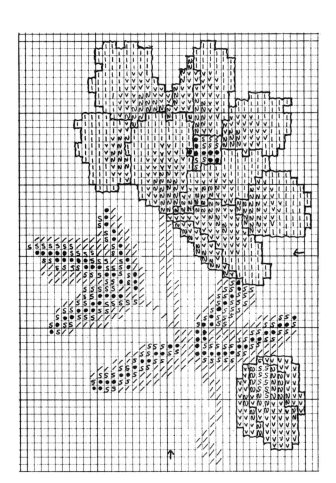

18 2¼ x 3¼
14 3 x 4¼

◀ **PEONY**
41 stitches by 59 stitches

BACK-STITCH	CROSS-STITCH	DMC #	
∿∿∿		310	black
	Ν	601	dark cranberry
	V	603	cranberry
	I	606	bright orange red
	●	700	bright Christmas green
	S	702	kelly green
	/	704	bright chartreuse

▼ **PANDA WITH BAMBOO**
40 stitches by 27 stitches

18 2¼ x 1½
14 2¾ x 2

BACK-STITCH	CROSS-STITCH	DMC #	
- - -	⊡		white
∿∿∿	●	310	black
	S	469	avocado green
	/	471	light avocado green
	Ν	701	light Christmas green
	L	704	bright chartreuse

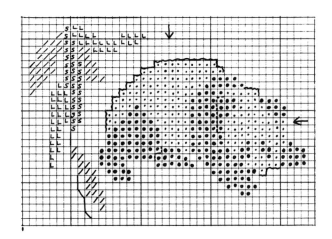

◀ **PEONY AND PLUM BLOSSOMS**
45 stitches by 47 stitches

BACK-STITCH	CROSS-STITCH	DMC #		or BALGER #8 BRAID	
∿∿∿		300	very dark mahogany		
	Ν	470	medium light avocado green		
	/	471	light avocado green		
———		729	medium old gold	002	gold
	+	740	tangerine		
	I	742	light tangerine		
	S	947	burnt orange		
	⊟	3350	very dark dusty rose		

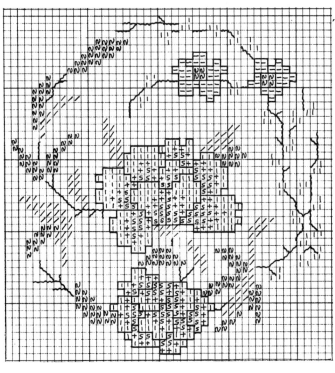

18 2½ x 2¾
14 3¼ x 3½

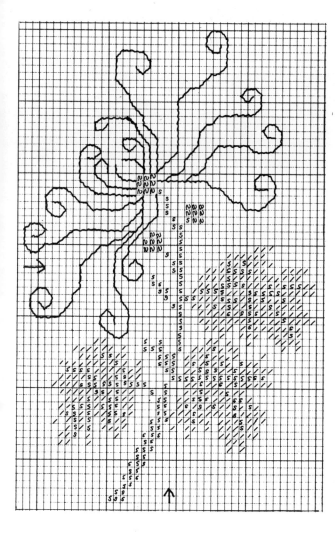

◄ **CHRYSANTHEMUM**

42 stitches by 66 stitches

BACK-STITCH	CROSS-STITCH	DMC #	
~~	Ⓝ	976	medium golden brown
	Ⓢ	3363	loden green
	Ⓩ	3364	light loden green

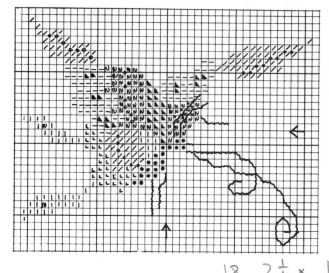

▲ **BUTTERFLY**

42 stitches by 32 stitches

18 2¼ × 1¾

14 3 × 2¼

FRENCH KNOT	BACK-STITCH	CROSS-STITCH	DMC #	
		Ⓛ	603	cranberry
		Ⓝ	666	bright Christmas red
		Ⓩ	704	bright chartreuse
		⊟	740	tangerine
∘		◣	806	dark peacock blue
	~~	●	815	medium garnet red
		Ⓘ	3766	light peacock blue

▼ **PANDA**

42 stitches by 23 stitches

BACK-STITCH	CROSS-STITCH	DMC #	
——	·		white
~~	●	310	black

▼ **NARROW BORDER**

18 stitch repeat by 5 stitches

BACK-STITCH	DMC #	
~~	310	black

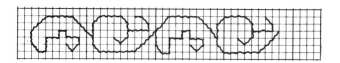

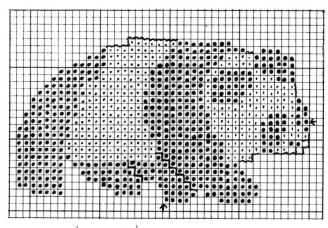

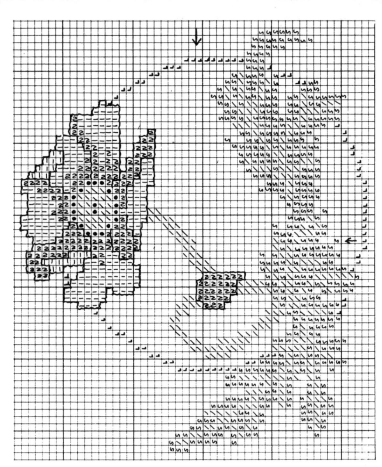

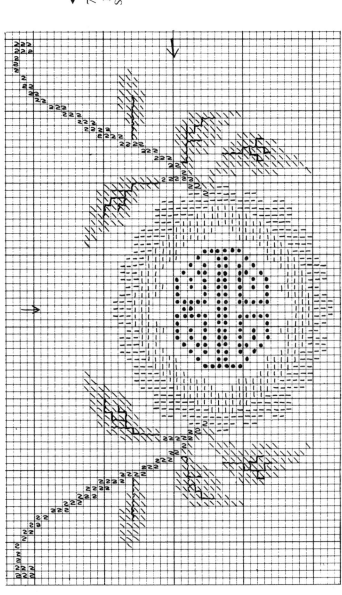

POPPY AND SUN ▶

59 stitches by 50 stitches

CROSS-STITCH		DMC #		or	BALGER #8 BRAID	
●		310	black			
I		351	coral			
S		469	avocado green			
I		666	bright Christmas red			
Z		704	bright chartreuse			
L		725	topaz		002	gold
N		815	medium garnet red			

BACK-STITCH ∿

18   $3\frac{1}{4}$ × $2\frac{3}{4}$

14   $4\frac{1}{4}$ × $3\frac{1}{2}$

▲ LONGEVITY

75 stitches by 46 stitches

CROSS-STITCH		DMC #		or	BALGER #8 BRAID	
●		310	black			
Z		580	dark moss green			
I		581	moss green			
I		725	topaz		002	gold
e		927	light gray blue		001	silver
		991	dark aquamarine			

BACK-STITCH ∿

18   $4\frac{1}{4}$ × $2\frac{1}{2}$

14   $5\frac{1}{2}$ × $3\frac{1}{4}$

▼ **MANDARIN DUCK AND FLOWERS**

76 stitches by 48 stitches

BACK-STITCH	CROSS-STITCH	DMC #	
	◢	310	black
		608	bright orange
	2	666	bright Christmas red
		742	light tangerine
	·	743	dark yellow
	6	747	very light sky blue
	●	991	dark aquamarine
	S	995	dark electric blue
	L	996	medium electric blue
	/	3761	light sky blue

18 4¼ × 2¾

14 5½ × 3½

14 3½ × 5

18 2½ × 4

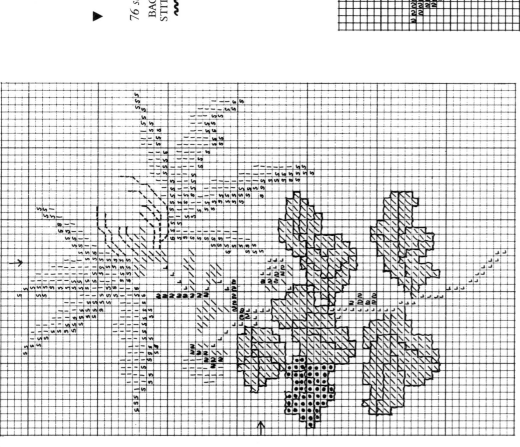

▲ **CHRYSANTHEMUM**

47 stitches by 71 stitches

BACK-STITCH	CROSS-STITCH	DMC #	
	●	300	very dark mahogany
	◹	400	dark mahogany
	2	469	avocado green
		608	bright orange
		729	medium old gold
	S	741	medium tangerine
	I	743	dark yellow
	L	904	very dark parrot green

or BALGER #8 BRAID

002 gold

LOTUS ▶

48 stitches by 57 stitches

BACK-STITCH	CROSS-STITCH	DMC #	
	⊥	604	light cranberry
	V	606	bright orange red
	⊘	704	bright chartreuse
	N	725	topaz

18   $2\frac{3}{4} \times 3\frac{1}{4}$

14   $3\frac{1}{2} \times 4\frac{1}{4}$

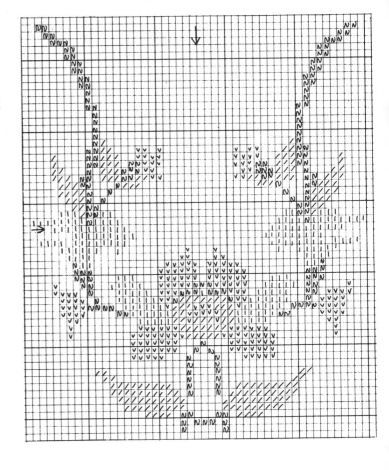

▼ BUTTERFLY BORDER

20 stitch repeat by 14 stitches

BACK-STITCH	CROSS-STITCH	DMC #	
	◉	517	dark Wedgwood blue
	✗	519	sky blue
	⊘	747	very light sky blue
﹏﹏	N	816	garnet red
	V	913	medium Nile green
	◉	957	pale geranium pink

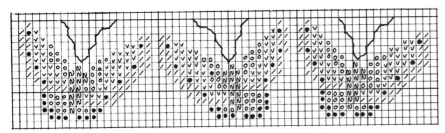

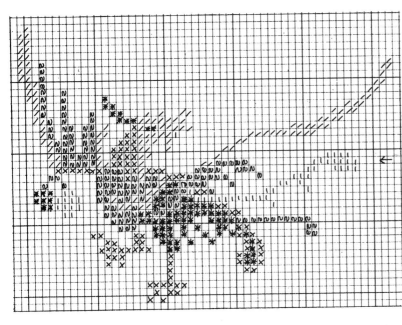

◀ PHOENIX

54 stitches by 39 stitches

	DMC #	
⊥	666	bright Christmas red
✗	782	medium topaz
✳	815	medium garnet red
⊘	958	dark aqua
N	996	medium electric blue

18   $3 \times 2\frac{1}{4}$

14   $3\frac{3}{4} \times 2\frac{3}{4}$

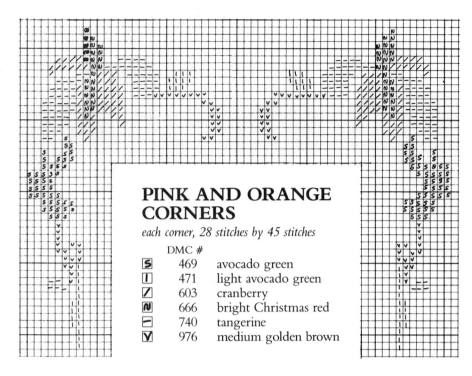

PINK AND ORANGE CORNERS

each corner, 28 stitches by 45 stitches

	DMC #	
S	469	avocado green
I	471	light avocado green
/	603	cranberry
N	666	bright Christmas red
–	740	tangerine
V	976	medium golden brown

ROOSTER ▶

38 stitches by 38 stitches

18   2¼ × 2¼
14   2¾ × 2¾

BACK-STITCH	CROSS-STITCH	DMC #	
	I	606	bright orange red
	●	943	medium aquamarine
	L	972	yellow orange
	·	973	bright canary yellow
∿∿∿	S	976	medium golden brown
	N	996	medium electric blue

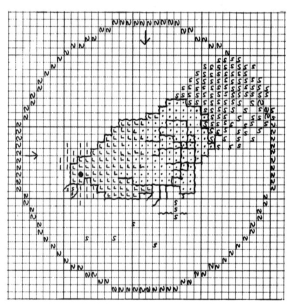

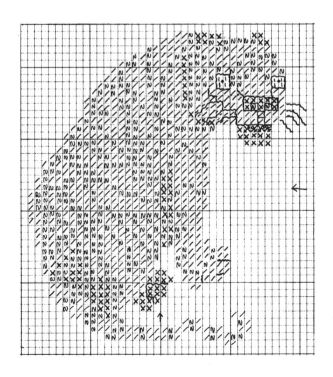

◀ TIGER

40 stitches by 44 stitches

FRENCH KNOT	BACK-STITCH	CROSS-STITCH	DMC #	
		o		white
•	∿∿∿	N	310	black
		I	726	light topaz
		X	780	very dark topaz
		/	783	Christmas gold

18   2¼ × 2½
14   2¾ × 3¼

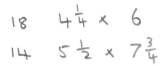

PHOENIX
76 stitches by 108 stitches

BACK-STITCH	CROSS-STITCH	DMC #	
	Z	666	bright Christmas red
	⊟	725	topaz
	P	780	very dark topaz
	L	806	dark peacock blue
	N	814	dark garnet red

BACK-STITCH	CROSS-STITCH	DMC #	
∿	●	825	dark blue
	S	909	very dark emerald green
	I	913	medium Nile green
	V	3766	light peacock blue

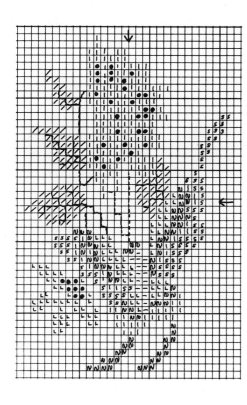

◀ BUTTERFLY AND FLOWERS

30 stitches by 47 stitches

BACK-STITCH	CROSS-STITCH	DMC #	
	L	604	light cranberry
	N	666	bright Christmas red
〜〜	●	699	Christmas green
	/	703	chartreuse
– – –	—	783	Christmas gold
	S	995	dark electric blue
	I	996	medium electric blue

18 $1\frac{3}{4} \times 2\frac{1}{2}$

14 $2\frac{1}{4} \times 3\frac{1}{2}$

▼ CAT

31 stitches by 54 stitches

18 $1\frac{3}{4} \times 3$

14 $2\frac{1}{4} \times 3\frac{3}{4}$

FRENCH KNOT	BACK-STITCH	CROSS-STITCH	DMC #	
		●		white
o	〜〜 —	●	310	black
			704	bright chartreuse
		N	931	medium antique blue
		/	932	light antique blue
		I	977	light golden brown

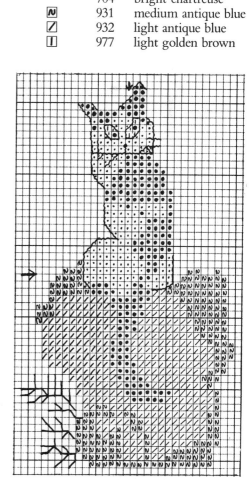

▼ BASKET OF FLOWERS

51 stitches by 38 stitches

	DMC #	
●	310	black
S	470	medium light avocado green
/	471	light avocado green
◤	580	dark moss green
I	666	bright Christmas red
X	725	topaz
N	816	garnet red
L	891	dark carnation pink
●	893	light carnation pink

18 $2\frac{3}{4} \times 2\frac{1}{4}$

14 $3\frac{1}{2} \times 2\frac{3}{4}$

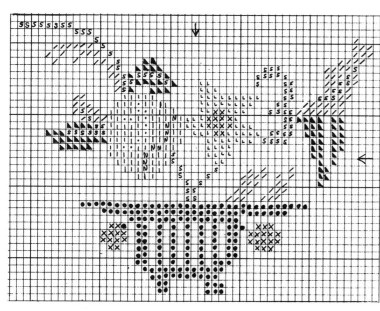

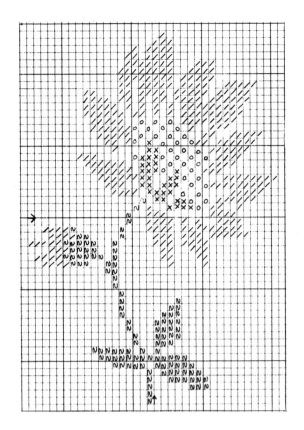

◄ CHRYSANTHEMUM AND BUD

36 stitches by 52 stitches

	DMC #	
☒	666	bright Christmas red
⊙	783	Christmas gold
ℕ	3685	dark mauve
⧄	3733	medium dusty rose

18   2 x 2¾

14   2½ x 3¾

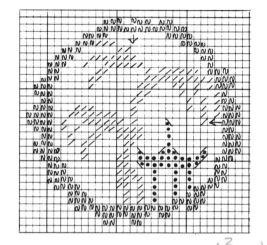

▲ PAVILION

31 stitches by 29 stitches

BACK-STITCH	CROSS-STITCH	DMC #	
——	●	310	black
	⧄	703	chartreuse
	ℕ	783	Christmas gold

18   1¾ x ½

14   2¼ x 2

▼ PHOENIX SINGING TO THE RISING SUN

73 stitches by 45 stitches

BACK-STITCH	CROSS-STITCH	DMC #	
——	ⓢ	666	bright Christmas red
- - -	ⓛ	702	kelly green
	Ⅰ	725	topaz
∿∿	ℕ	995	dark electric blue
	⧄	996	medium electric blue
	⊟	3766	light peacock blue

18   4 x 2½

14   5¼ x 3¼

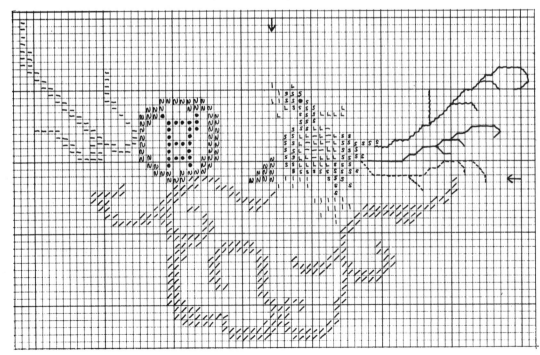

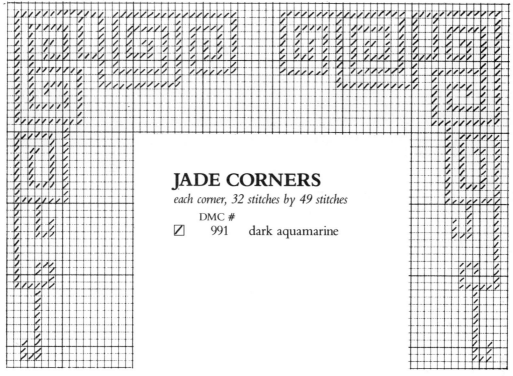

JADE CORNERS

each corner, 32 stitches by 49 stitches

DMC #

☑ 991 dark aquamarine

GOLD BORDER ▶

23 stitch repeat by 20 stitches

	DMC #		or	BALGER #8 BRAID
☑	725	topaz		002	gold

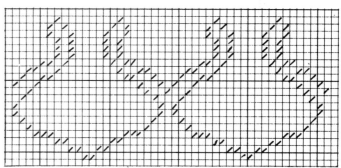

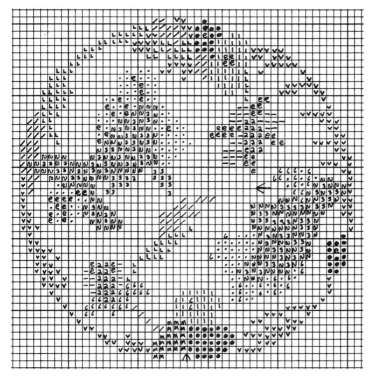

◀ TWO GOLDFISH

48 stitches by 48 stitches

	DMC #	
☑	471	light avocado green
V	518	light Wedgwood blue
2	603	cranberry
N	606	bright orange red
e	608	bright orange
L	702	kelly green
6	740	tangerine
3	742	light tangerine
•	743	dark yellow
⌐	899	medium rose
●	926	medium gray blue
M	3752	very light antique blue
I	3761	light sky blue

18 $2\frac{3}{4} \times 2\frac{3}{4}$

14 $3\frac{1}{2} \times 3\frac{1}{2}$

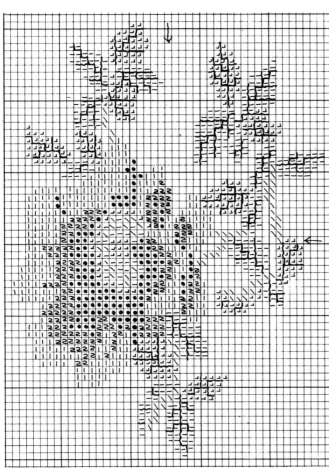

GOLDFISH

62 stitches by 51 stitches

$18 \quad 3\frac{1}{2} \times 2\frac{3}{4}$

$14 \quad 4\frac{1}{2} \times 3\frac{1}{2}$

BACK-STITCH	CROSS-STITCH	DMC #	
	●	310	black
	◨	349	dark coral
	I	352	light coral
	✕	519	sky blue
	▽	581	moss green
	◣	725	topaz
	◰	816	garnet red
	L	948	very light peach
		3761	light sky blue

———

〰〰

POPPY ▶

61 stitches by 45 stitches

$18 \quad 3\frac{1}{2} \times 2\frac{1}{2}$

$14 \quad 4\frac{1}{2} \times 3\frac{1}{4}$

BACK-STITCH	CROSS-STITCH	DMC #	
	◨	353	peach
	L	580	dark moss green
	◩	606	bright orange red
	◿	704	bright chartreuse
	●	816	garnet red
		936	very dark avocado green
	I	992	aquamarine

〰〰

32

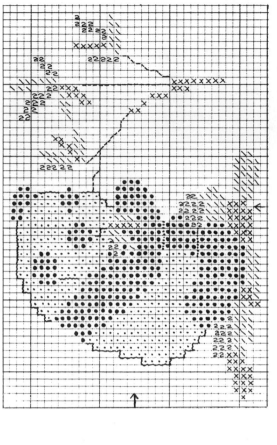

▲ PANDA

54 stitches by 36 stitches

18   3 × 2

14   3 3/4 × 2 1/2

BACK-STITCH	CROSS-STITCH	DMC #	
⋯⋯	⊡		white
∿∿	⬤	310	black
	Z	580	dark moss green
– –	✗	700	bright Christmas green
	∕	704	bright chartreuse

▲ BLUEBIRD

53 stitches by 36 stitches

18   3 × 2

14   3 3/4 × 2 1/2

BACK-STITCH	CROSS-STITCH	DMC #	
	⬤	310	black
	∕	471	light avocado green
	S	666	bright Christmas red
	∨	725	topaz
	○	726	light topaz
	✗	783	Christmas gold
	◣	796	dark royal blue
	▯	807	medium peacock blue
	Z	991	dark aquamarine
∿∿	◀	3031	very dark mocha brown

▼ ORANGE AND BLUE BORDER

69 stitch repeat by 14 stitches

	DMC #	
⬤	310	black
∕	608	bright orange
✗	666	bright Christmas red
S	700	bright Christmas green
L	958	dark aqua

33

FLYING PHOENIX

76 stitches by 107 stitches

BACK-STITCH	CROSS-STITCH	DMC #		BACK-STITCH	CROSS-STITCH	DMC #	
6		349	dark coral	〰〰	A	729	medium old gold
/		352	light coral		X	783	Christmas gold
•		699	Christmas green		S	816	garnet red
N		702	kelly green		�£	995	dark electric blue
V		704	bright chartreuse		L	996	medium electric blue
=		725	topaz		I	3761	light sky blue

18 $4\frac{1}{4}$ × 6

14 $5\frac{1}{2}$ × $7\frac{3}{4}$

34

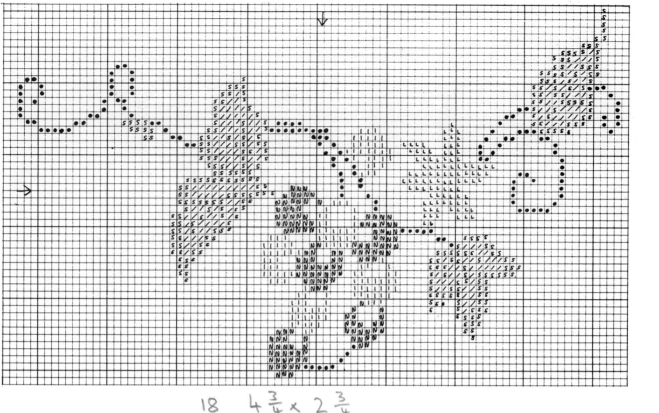

18   4 $\frac{3}{4}$ x 2 $\frac{3}{4}$

14   6 $\frac{1}{4}$ x 3 $\frac{3}{4}$

▲ GRAPES

87 stitches by 52 stitches

	DMC #	
N	327	dark gray violet
I	340	medium lilac
Z	368	light pistachio green
●	469	avocado green
L	666	bright Christmas red
S	958	dark aqua

18 4 $\frac{3}{4}$ x 2 $\frac{1}{2}$

14 6 $\frac{1}{4}$ x 3 $\frac{1}{4}$

▼ GOLDEN LANDSCAPE

86 stitches by 46 stitches

BACK-STITCH	CROSS-STITCH	DMC #		or BALGER #8 BRAID	
∿∿	●	310	black		
	Z	725	topaz	002	gold

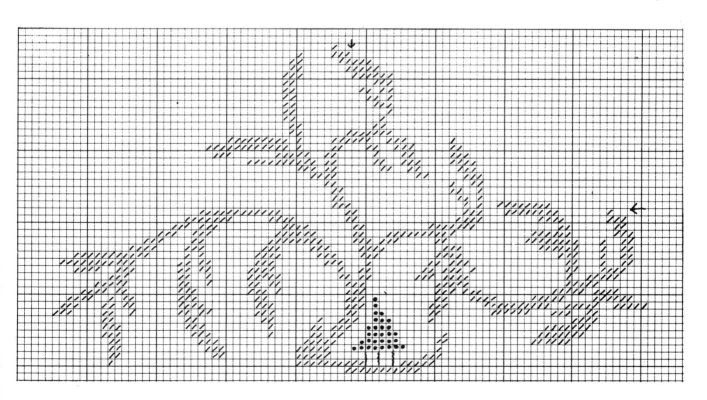

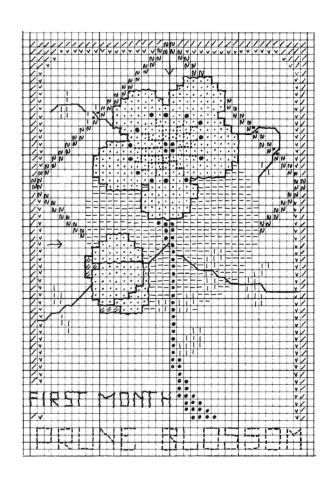

FIRST MONTH
PRUNE BLOSSOM

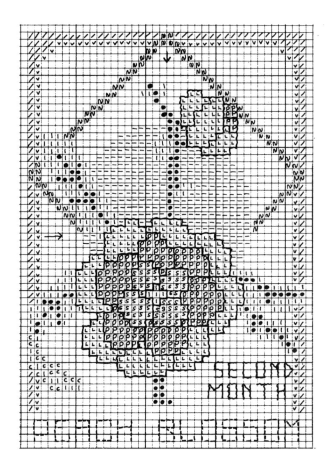

SECOND MONTH
PEACH BLOSSOM

THIRD MONTH
TREE PEONY

TWELVE MONTHS
each, 40 stitches by 57 stitches

BACK-STITCH	CROSS-STITCH	DMC #	
	⊡		white
〰	◣	310	black
	S	335	rose
	⧰	415	pearl gray
– – –	N	666	bright Christmas red
——	●	699	Christmas green
⋯⋯	I	701	light Christmas green
	C	704	bright chartreuse
	V	725	topaz
	⊟	726	light topaz
	6	740	tangerine
	φ	742	light tangerine
	L	776	medium pink
	⧄	806	dark peacock blue
	P	899	medium rose
	U	3766	light peacock blue

18ct 2¼ x 3¼

14ct 2¾ x 4

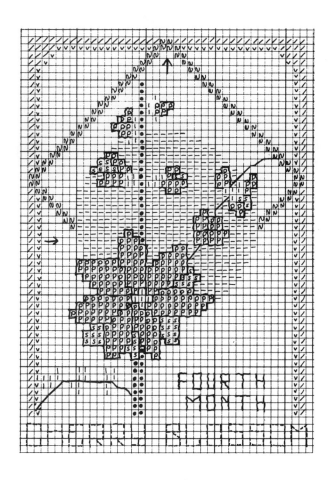

FOURTH
MONTH

CHERRY BLOSSOM

FIFTH MONTH

MAGNOLIA

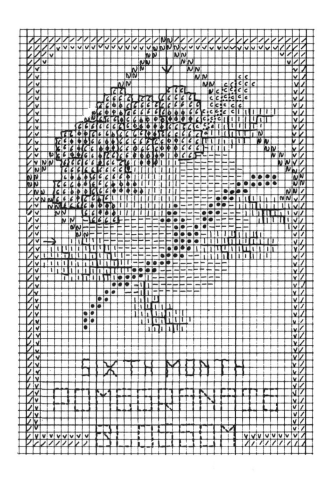

SIXTH MONTH

POMEGRANATE

BLOSSOM

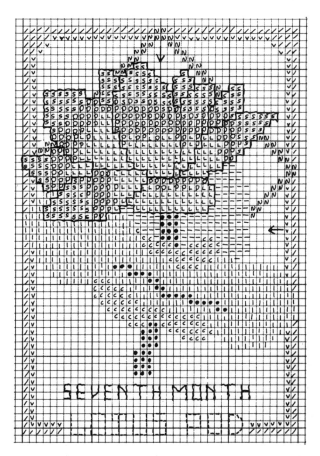

SEVENTH MONTH

LOTUS BUD

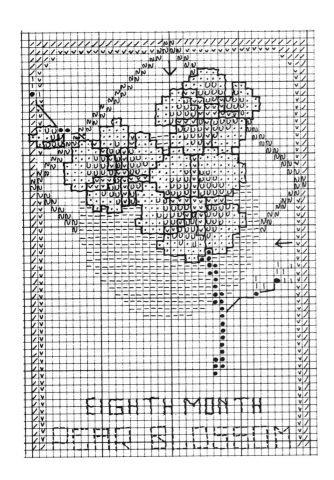

EIGHTH MONTH
PEAR BLOSSOM

NINTH MONTH
MALLOW

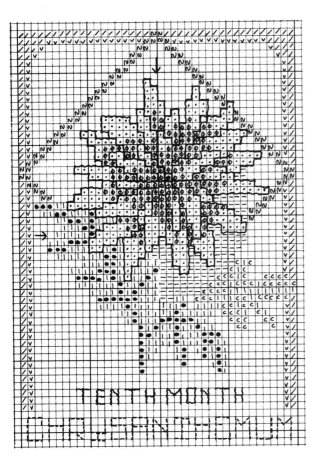

TENTH MONTH
CHRYSANTHEMUM

TWELVE MONTHS

each, 40 stitches by 57 stitches

BACK-STITCH	CROSS-STITCH	DMC #	
	⊡		white
∿∿∿	◼	310	black
	S	335	rose
	⁄⁄	415	pearl gray
– – –	N	666	bright Christmas red
——	●	699	Christmas green
······	I	701	light Christmas green
	C	704	bright chartreuse
	V	725	topaz
	⊟	726	light topaz
	6	740	tangerine
	φ	742	light tangerine
	L	776	medium pink
	⁄	806	dark peacock blue
	P	899	medium rose
	U	3766	light peacock blue

18ct   2¼ × 3¼

14ct   2¾ × 4

ELEVENTH MONTH
GARDENIA

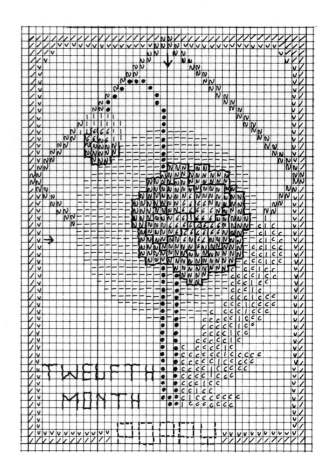

TWELFTH
MONTH
HOLLY

VASE OF FLOWERS ▶

27 stitches by 32 stitches

18 1½ × 1¾

14 2 × 2¼

BACK-STITCH	CROSS-STITCH	DMC #	
——	Ͷ	469	avocado green
	●	518	light Wedgwood blue
	◿	519	sky blue
	∐	603	cranberry
	✕	606	bright orange red
	∟	702	kelly green
～～～	◣	816	garnet red

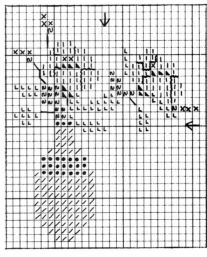

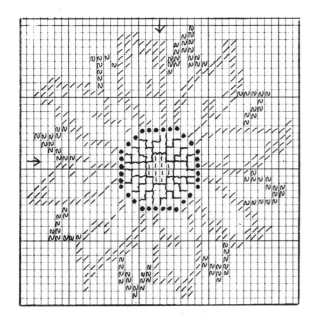

◀ SUNBURST

38 stitches by 38 stitches

18 2¼ × 2¼

14 2¾ × 2¾

BACK-STITCH	CROSS-STITCH	DMC #	
～～～	∐	666	bright Christmas red
	◿	725	topaz
	Ͷ	783	Christmas gold
	●	815	medium garnet red

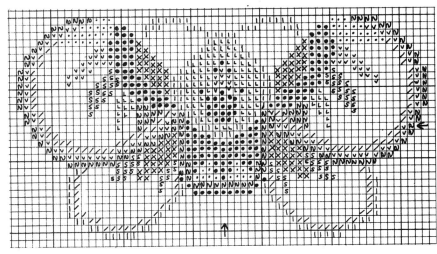

◄ LARGE BUTTERFLY

59 stitches by 31 stitches

	DMC #	
L	608	bright orange
N	666	bright Christmas red
/	704	bright chartreuse
S	740	tangerine
V	742	light tangerine
·	743	dark yellow
●	816	garnet red
I	958	dark aqua
X	995	dark electric blue

18 $3\frac{1}{4} \times 1\frac{3}{4}$

14 $4\frac{1}{4} \times 2\frac{1}{4}$

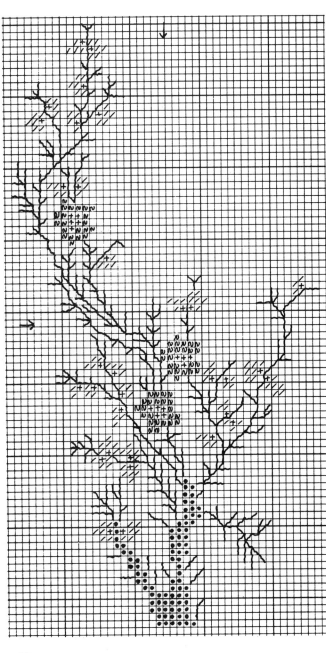

◄ PLUM BLOSSOMS

44 stitches by 84 stitches

BACK-STITCH	CROSS-STITCH	DMC #		Anchor
	/	210	medium lavender	104
∿∿	●	327	dark gray violet	100
	+	603	cranberry	62
	N	666	bright Christmas red	46

18 $2\frac{1}{2} \times 4\frac{3}{4}$

14 $3\frac{1}{4} \times 6$

PHOENIX AND FLOWERS ►

84 stitches by 117 stitches

BACK-STITCH	CROSS-STITCH	DMC #	
	M	340	medium lilac
∿∿		550	very dark violet
	◣	552	dark violet
	V	554	light violet
	▲	601	dark cranberry
	⊟	604	light cranberry
	6	606	bright orange red
	I	701	light Christmas green
	/	702	kelly green
	+	704	bright chartreuse
	L	740	tangerine
	●	796	dark royal blue
	·	927	light gray blue
	N	976	medium golden brown
	X	3761	light sky blue
	II	3765	very dark peacock blue

18 $4\frac{3}{4} \times 6\frac{1}{2}$

14 $6 \times 8\frac{1}{2}$

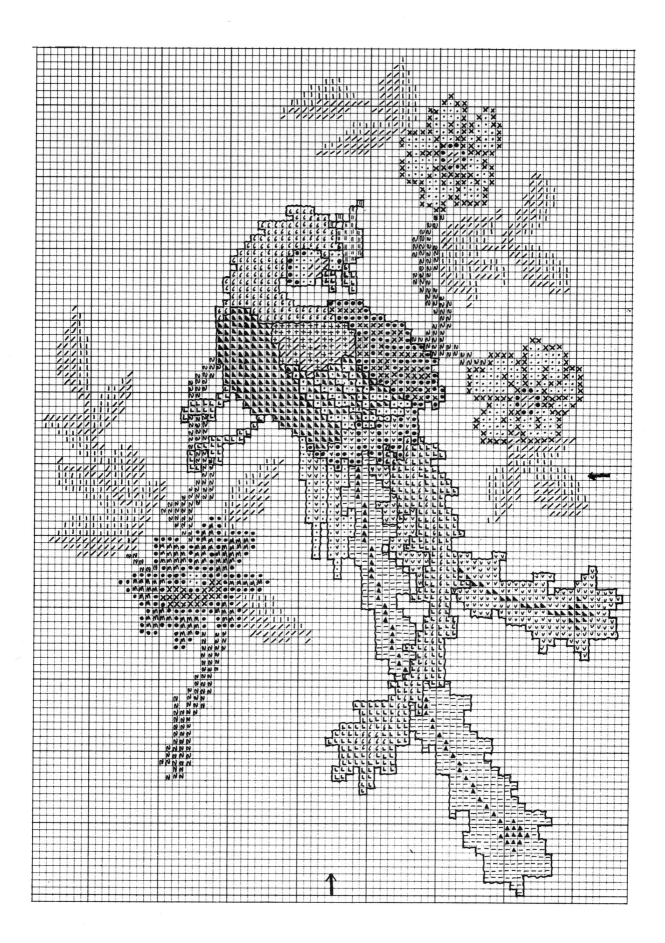

GREEN DRAGON ✻ round

91 stitches by 109 stitches

	DMC #	
◿	319	very dark pistachio green
L	320	medium pistachio green
6	367	dark pistachio green
·	368	light pistachio green
⊟	603	cranberry
✕	666	bright Christmas red
I	725	topaz
Ͷ	815	medium garnet red
Ⴘ	3761	light sky blue

18 ct   5 x 6
14 ct   6½ x 7¾

▲ CRANE

79 stitches by 51 stitches

BACK-STITCH	CROSS-STITCH	DMC #	
	⊡		white
– – –		310	black
	Ⓝ	666	bright Christmas red
	⧄	991	dark aquamarine
	Ⅱ	992	aquamarine

18    $4\frac{1}{2} \times 2\frac{3}{4}$

14    $5\frac{3}{4} \times 3\frac{1}{2}$

▼ LATTICE BORDER

18 stitch repeat by 19 stitches

	DMC #	
Ⅱ	666	bright Christmas red
⧄	725	topaz
Ⓝ	995	dark electric blue

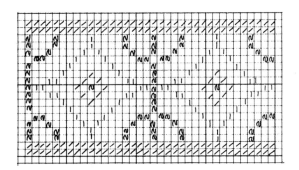

▼ FIVE BATS AND LONGEVITY

41 stitches by 41 stitches

	DMC #		or	BALGER #8 BRAID	
Ⓝ	498	dark Christmas red			
⧄	725	topaz		002	gold
⊡	924	very dark gray blue			
Ⓢ	926	medium gray blue			
Ⅱ	928	very light gray blue			

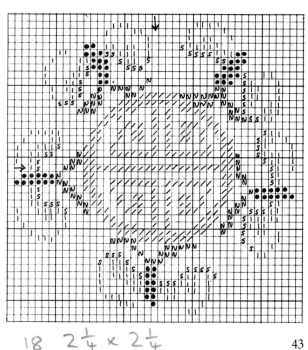

18    $2\frac{1}{4} \times 2\frac{1}{4}$

14   3×3

43

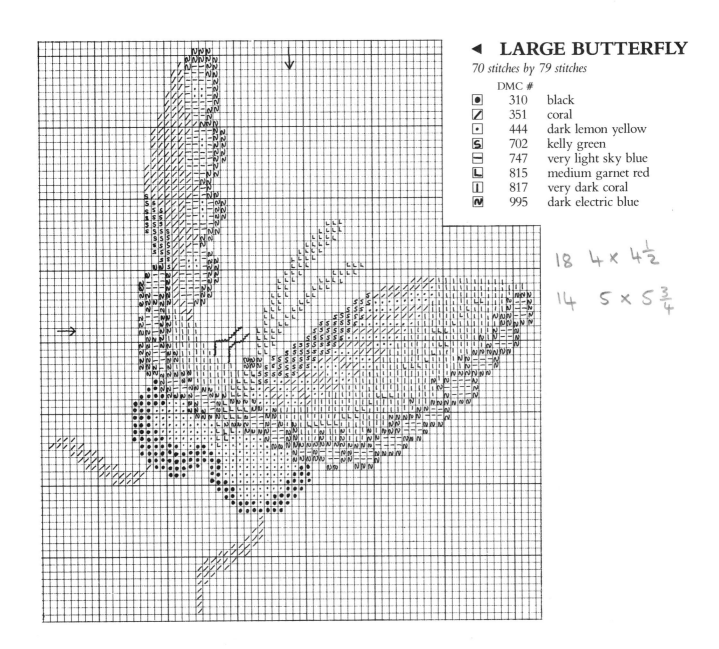

70 stitches by 79 stitches

	DMC #	
⊙	310	black
⊘	351	coral
·	444	dark lemon yellow
S	702	kelly green
⊟	747	very light sky blue
L	815	medium garnet red
I	817	very dark coral
N	995	dark electric blue

18 4 × 4½

14 5 × 5¾

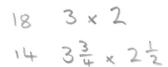

18 3 × 2

14 3¾ × 2½

PEONY WITH BUD ►

52 stitches by 35 stitches

BACK-STITCH	CROSS-STITCH	DMC #	
	⊡		white
∿		601	dark cranberry
	I	603	cranberry
	L	605	very light cranberry
– – –	S	991	dark aquamarine
	⊘	992	aquamarine
	N	3765	very dark peacock blue

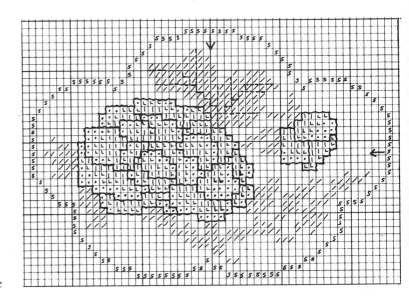

44

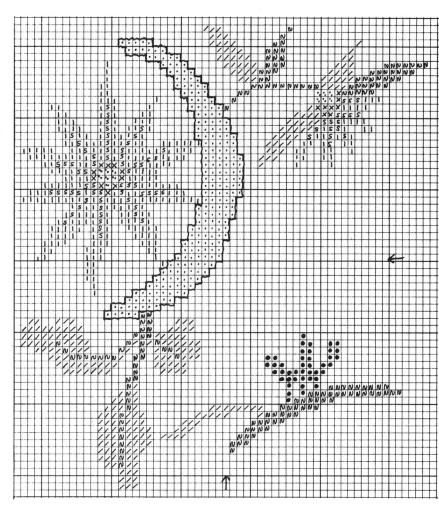

18 $3\frac{1}{4} \times 3\frac{3}{4}$

14 $4\frac{1}{4} \times 4\frac{1}{2}$

▲ **NEW MOON**

59 stitches by 65 stitches

BACK-STITCH	CROSS-STITCH	DMC #		or	BALGER #8 BRAID	
	⊡		white		032	pearl
	⬤	310	black			
	N	701	light Christmas green			
	∕	704	bright chartreuse			
	X	740	tangerine			
	⠉	743	dark yellow			
	S	806	dark peacock blue			
∿∿∿		3765	very dark peacock blue			
	I	3766	light peacock blue			

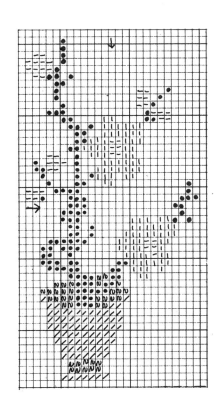

◀ **VASE OF PLUM BLOSSOMS**

25 stitches by 48 stitches

	DMC #	
⊟	209	dark lavender
I	893	light carnation pink
⬤	975	dark golden brown
N	995	dark electric blue
∕	996	medium electric blue

18 $1\frac{1}{2} \times 2\frac{3}{4}$

14 $1\frac{3}{4} \times 3\frac{1}{2}$

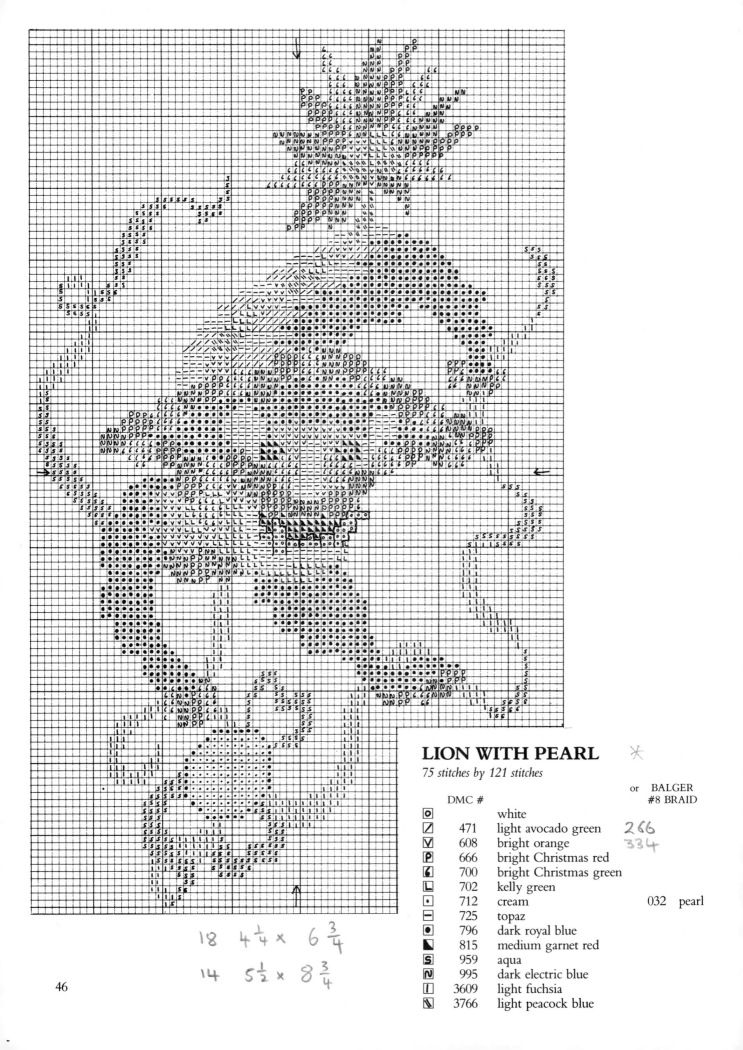

LION WITH PEARL ✳
75 stitches by 121 stitches

	DMC #		or BALGER #8 BRAID
▢		white	
◪	471	light avocado green	266
⊽	608	bright orange	334
�ℙ	666	bright Christmas red	
⌈	700	bright Christmas green	
⌊	702	kelly green	
·	712	cream	032 pearl
⊟	725	topaz	
●	796	dark royal blue	
◣	815	medium garnet red	
S	959	aqua	
N	995	dark electric blue	
I	3609	light fuchsia	
◺	3766	light peacock blue	

18 $4\frac{1}{4}$ × $6\frac{3}{4}$

14 $5\frac{1}{2}$ × $8\frac{3}{4}$

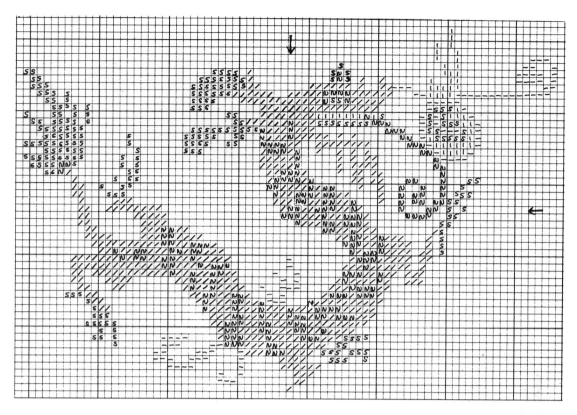

▲ BLUE DRAGON

77 stitches by 51 stitches

18 4¼ × 2¾

14 5½ × 3¾

	DMC #	
Ⴖ	606	bright orange red
Ⅰ	726	light topaz
S	995	dark electric blue
∕	996	medium electric blue
⊟	3761	light sky blue

▼ FLOWER AND FIGURE BORDER

22 stitch repeat by 27 stitches

BACK-STITCH	CROSS-STITCH	DMC #	
〜〜〜	●	310	black
	Ⅰ	518	light Wedgwood blue
......	Ⴖ	666	bright Christmas red
	∕	704	bright chartreuse
	⊡	725	topaz

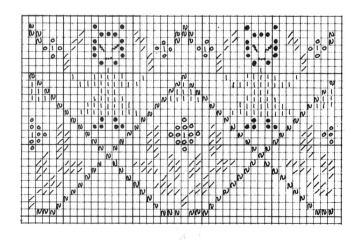

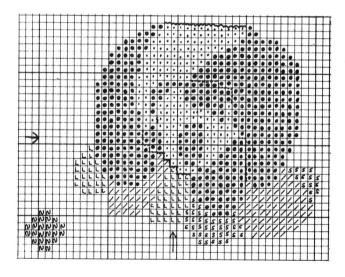

▲ PANDA PLAYING

43 stitches by 32 stitches

18 2½ × 1¾

14 3 × 2¼

BACK-STITCH	CROSS-STITCH	DMC #	
---	·		white
〜〜〜	●	310	black
	S	469	avocado green
	Ⴖ	666	bright Christmas red
	L	701	light Christmas green
	∕	704	bright chartreuse

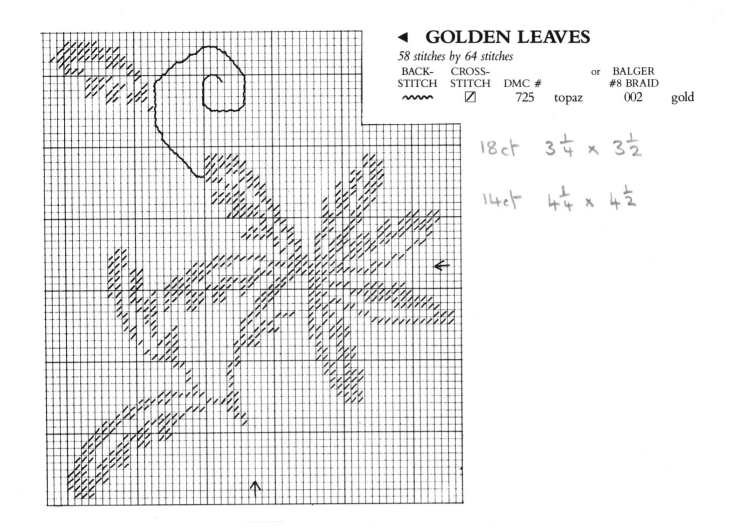

◄ **GOLDEN LEAVES**

58 stitches by 64 stitches

BACK-STITCH	CROSS-STITCH	DMC #		or	BALGER #8 BRAID	
〜〜〜	⧄	725	topaz		002	gold

18ct $3\frac{1}{4} \times 3\frac{1}{2}$

14ct $4\frac{1}{4} \times 4\frac{1}{2}$

BUTTERFLY AND FLOWER ▶

18 3 × 3

14 4 × 4

56 stitches by 56 stitches

BACK-STITCH	CROSS-STITCH	DMC #	
	☑	470	medium light avocado green
– – –	⊡	580	dark moss green
	☒	606	bright orange red
〜〜〜	◨	701	light Christmas green
	⧄	704	bright chartreuse
	⊟	725	topaz
	⊡	726	light topaz
	L	747	very light sky blue
	6	780	very dark topaz
	N	815	medium garnet red
	S	893	light carnation pink
	I	894	very light carnation pink

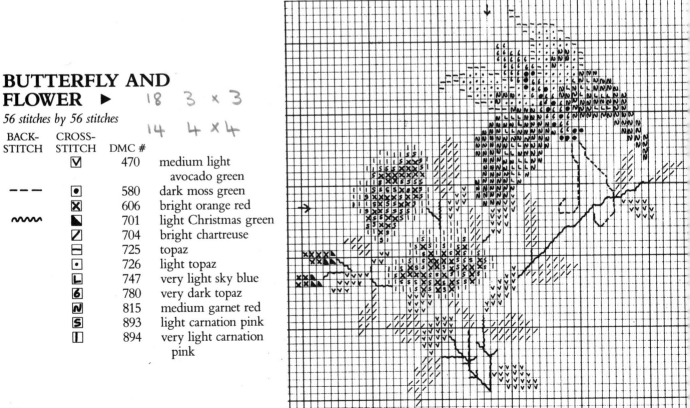